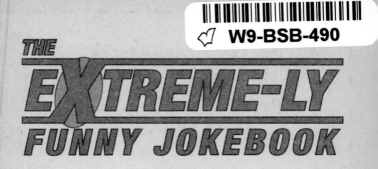

THE EXTREME-LY FUNNY JOKEBOOK

by Chris Tait

Incorporated

Copyright © 2002 Kidsbooks, Inc.
230 Fifth Avenue
New York, NY 10001

Manufactured in Canada

Why don't snowboarders make good plumbers?

Because they only know about half-pipes!

☆

What do you call the biggest skateboarder in the world?

Ollie-phant!

☆

Why are skateboarders so cheap about buying clothes?

Because they believe in free style!

☆

Why are inline skaters so excited?

Because they never feel board!

What is a bungee jumper's favorite part of a song?

The bridge!

Knock, knock!
Who's there?
Caddy!
Caddy who?
Caddy ya own surfboard, dude!

What is a snowboarder's favorite type of vegetation?

The hand plant!

❀☆❀

How do snowboarders face a hill?

Nose first!

❀☆❀

What did the gloomy snowboarder say when he got off the lift?

It's all downhill from here!

❀☆❀

Why did the extreme surfer think that the sea was his friend?

Because it gave him a big wave as he went by!

❀☆❀

What did the boarders call the girl who loved to do 360s?

Mary-Go-Round!

What advice did the white-water kayaker give as she went over the rapid?

Roll with it!

Why did the skydiver feel a little nervous during his jump?

Because he had that old sinking feeling!

What did the extreme biker call her winter wheels?

Her ice cycle!

Why did the skateboarder pick up speed going downhill?

Because he had an inclination to go faster!

ᗧ☆ᗤ

What do you call the guy who is the world's best on the half-pipe?

The chairman of the board!

ᗧ☆ᗤ

Why don't they build skate parks in outer space?

Because you can't get any air there!

ᗧ☆ᗤ

What did the BMXer say when she crashed into the straw?

I guess it's time to hit the hay!

What do you call a surfer who only wants to board in Rio?

Brazil nuts!

Knock, knock!
Who's there?
Canoe!
Canoe who?
Canoe help me wax my surfboard?

What do you call the best extreme skier?

Snow Wonder!

What do snowboarders do when they have an itch?

Pull a backscratcher!

☆

Knock, knock!
Who's there?
Ida!
Ida who?
Ida like to learn how to ride a BMX bike!

☆

What do BMXers love to do around Easter?

Bunny hops!

☆

What do pro skateboarders love about their jobs?

The everyday grind!

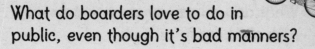

What do boarders love to do in public, even though it's bad manners?

The Nosepick!

☆

Why did the boarder think she could fly?

Because she was wearing her Airwalks!

☆

Why don't Aussies get sleepy on the waves?

Because they're all wake boarding!

☆

Why is inline trick skating like flying a plane?

Because all anyone remembers is the landing!

What do you say when an extreme rock climber almost falls?

Get a grip!

☆

What did the boarder's friend say when she saw him wipe out?

Looks like he's going to get that much-needed break!

☆

What happened when the BMXer landed the giant jump?

She got a big shock!

☆

Why couldn't the silly man use his new water skis?

He was searching for a lake with a slope!

What did the surfer think of the wave that he saw coming up in front of him?

He thought it was swell!

What did the experienced surfer say about the youngster who got stranded?

Paddle teach him!

Why do boarders love Thanksgiving?

It's a good chance to practice their carving!

🐝☆🐝

Knock, knock!
Who's there?
Wanda!
Wanda who?
Wanda teach me how to snowboard?

🐝☆🐝

What kind of music do surfers like best?

New wave, of course!

🐝☆🐝

What dance do boarders go to every winter?

The Snowball!

Why do bikers get upset when they have to do the dishes?

Because they worry about their forks all the time!

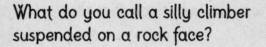

What does a BMXer call his posse?

The Chain Gang!

What do you call a silly climber suspended on a rock face?

Dope on a rope!

What do you call a climber scrambling to keep her grip on the mountain?

Grope on a rope!

What do you call a climbing line
hanging over a cliff?

Rope on a slope!

How did the climber get to the top of
the mountain before everyone else?

He sneaked a peak!

Do most climbers think that they
will fall?

Knot if they can help it!

What do climbers and plastic wrap
have in common?

They both know how to cling on!

Why don't skydivers like port-able phones?

Because they don't believe in going cordless!

What did the polite skydiver say when her pack didn't open?

Chute!

Why do snowboarders make such bad farmers?

Because they hate to "bail"!

How do the snorkelers know when it's dinnertime?

They hear the diving bell!

🐚⭐🐚

What do divers use to take photos under the water?

A fish-eye lens, of course!

🐚⭐🐚

Why did the surfer cross the water?

To get to the other tide!

🐚⭐🐚

What was the saddest animal the diver had ever seen?

The blue whale!

🐚⭐🐚

What do skaters like that boxers hate?

A fat lip!

🌀☆🌀

What does one wear to a surfer's wedding?

A good wetsuit!

🌀☆🌀

Knock, knock!
Who's there?
Indy!
Indy who?
Indy mood to go surfing?

🌀☆🌀

What kind of music do deep-sea divers love?

Sole music!

What do skaters have in common with Fred Flintstone?

They all like to go bowling!

When should you never let a BMXer stay over at your house?

When she asks if she can crash on your couch!

What is a BMXer's worst enemy?

Gravity!

Why are boarders such dreamers?

Because they never want to come back down to earth!

What is the worst thing you can say when punishing an inline trick skater?

You're grounded!

Why are surfers great gamblers?

Because they know when to let it ride!

What is it called when a wave is so big that a surfer doesn't stop until he hits the grass?

Surf and turf!

What is the one hairstyle surfers don't mind having?

A permanent wave!

How do you work out to train for the big wave?

Practice rip curls!

☆

How do extreme surfers greet each other?

Hey, Haw-ai-i?

☆

What do extreme ski jumpers love most about their car stereos?

The aerials!

☆

Why didn't the silly man use his new cross-country skis?

He was searching for a very small country!

How did the extreme jumper show that he was excited?

He flipped out!

How did the reckless skier get rid of her extra gear?

She had a yard sale!

When you take the big jump, what are your rhyming choices mid-air?

Sail or bail!

How did the musician board on the big hill?

She was afraid that she'd B flat!

How did the bummed-out boarder pick himself up?

He got on the chair lift!

Why were the surfers happy to hear that a storm was coming?

Because they thought it was a wind-wind situation!

Who won when the climbers raced to make the quickest knot?

It was a tie!

⁓☆⁓

Why was the climbing movie split into two parts?

Because it was a cliff-hanger!

⁓☆⁓

What did the diver say when his friend asked how his diving trip went?

Swimmingly!

⁓☆⁓

How did the surfer feel after a whole weekend on the sunny sea?

Burned out!

⁓☆⁓

What did the inline skater say after crashing down the hill?

Give me a brake!

🐝☆🐝

Knock, knock!
Who's there?
Claire!
Claire who?
Claire the way, I'm coming down the hill!

🐝☆🐝

What do you call an inline skater who crashes and burns?

A trailblazer!

🐝☆🐝

How do you say good-bye to an inline fanatic?

Later, Skater!

What did the inline skater say when she got lost in the skate shop?

I can't seem to get my bearings!

⚡☆⚡

What is the inline skater's motto?

Roll with it!

⚡☆⚡

How did the boarder make the hill angry?

He just kept crossing it!

⚡☆⚡

What did the inline skater say to his buddy when he saw dogs chasing them?

Don't look now, but I think we're being tailed!

What did the dentist say to
the skater?

**I want you to stop
grinding your teeth!**

What part of the inline skate can you
never trust?

The heel!

Why do inline skates seem so rude?

**Because they always stick
out their tongues!**

What do you get when you rewind your skate-tricks video?

Some wicked backslides!

🌀☆🌀

What do boarders have in common with martial artists?

They both love the kick flip!

🌀☆🌀

What do boarders have in common with the big rig riders?

They all love their trucks!

🌀☆🌀

What is the worst part about racing downhill against the clock?

The time is always running down!

What did the boarders say when they were playing hide and seek?

Ollie, Ollie, oxen free!

☆

Why do some skaters' faces look so nasty?

Because of their noseblunts!

☆

Why did the BMXer have a shower halfway through the race?

He wanted to make a clean break!

☆

Why are skaters so bummed out?

Because they're always doing the downhill slide!

What did the first-time skier say
about his first day on the slope?

**By the time I learned to stand
up, I couldn't sit down!**

Knock, knock!
Who's there?
Mick!
Mick who?
McTwist!

Why are boarders so good at division?

**Because they always know
what half a 360 is!**

What is the worst part about falling
on the steps when you're boarding?

Bailing on the railing!

Why do windsurfers hate pollution so much?

Because they love to get good air!

☆

What did the hang glider say after his first run?

That was pretty good for a first draft!

☆

What do you call a skate trick from Louisiana?

'Nawlins N'ollie!

☆

Why do snowboarders hate to be at the back of a plane?

Because it's harder to catch frontside air!

What food do inline skaters hate?

Road pizza!

🐝☆🐝

Why are deep-sea divers so tense?

They're under a lot of pressure!

🐝☆🐝

How do big-wave hunters learn
the rules?

They go to the surfboard!

🐝☆🐝

Where do surfers learn to dance?

On boogie boards!

🐝☆🐝

What do Hawaiian surfers do when
they're tired?

They lei down!

What did the shark say to the surfer when it chomped on her board?

I just stopped by for a bite!

What is a shark's favorite meal?

Surf and turf!

What do surfers not mind seeing breaking?

Waves!

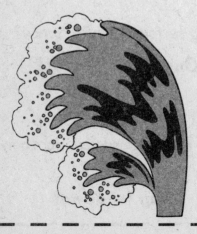

What type of vegetation do snow-boarders hate?

Face plants!

🌀⭐🌀

What does a mountain climber have in common with a map?

They both work to scale!

🌀⭐🌀

How did the mountain biker approach the hill?

He got all geared up about it!

🌀⭐🌀

What do mountain bikers call apartments where they stop to rest?

Their brake pads!

🌀⭐🌀

What do mountain bikers call the helmets that protect their heads?

Brain buckets!

What is the smelliest part of a mountain biking race?

De-scent!

What did the other racers call the team from Finland?

The Finnish line!

How do extreme mountain bikers feel about broken pedals?

A little cranky!

Why are trick riders so high-strung?

**Because they're a
little jumpy!**

Where do mountain bikers look for
classifieds?

In the ad-venture!

What do extreme bikers think of riding
through bear country?

It's grizzly!

Knock, knock!
Who's there?
Al!
Al who?
Alpine skiing!

How did the hang glider feel after sailing for an hour through a storm?

A little winded!

⊰☆⊱

What did the rider get after doing the tough course in the rain?

An obsta-cold!

⊰☆⊱

What do big-mountain snowboarders call December to February?

Peak season!

⊰☆⊱

What did the mountain biker do after her bike collided with another bike tire?

They spoke about it for a while!

What do bikers call their annual scrapbooks?

The gearbook!

᙭☆᙭

What did the biker do when he realized he had insulted someone?

He really had to back-pedal!

᙭☆᙭

What did the windsurfer think of the flashy new guy who couldn't turn?

She thought he lacked tack!

How did the windsurfer get his gear so cheap?

It was on sail!

⚡☆⚡

What did the diver have to say after the great wedding ceremony?

There wasn't a dry suit in the house!

⚡☆⚡

What is a windsurfer's favorite candy?

Life Savers, of course!

⚡☆⚡

What did the one skater say about his friend's great Ollie story?

Sounds like a tall tail to me!

⚡☆⚡

What do skaters call it when they skate to school with their lunches?

Meals on wheels!

🐝☆🐝

What makes skaters so curious?

They practice sticking their noses in everything!

🐝☆🐝

What is the worst part about boarding before the season starts?

The climb to the top!

🐝☆🐝

What did the announcer say when she saw the two kayakers in a close finish?

I don't know if it's one oar the other!

What did the kayaker say when the beginner said that he could beat him?

Paddle be the day!

What do boarders and cowboys have in common?

Rodeo flips!

When is a snowboard like an old piano?

When it needs to be tuned!

How did the boarder get rid of her dullness?

She sharpened her board!

What are the only commitments most boarders believe in?

Bindings!

☆

How did the boarder feel when he saw how much his new wraparounds cost?

He was goggle boggled!

☆

How did the skier decide to hide her skiing buddy's gear?

She took a pole!

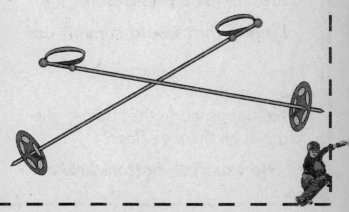

What did the extreme skier get his fiancée on the night of their engagement?

A black diamond!

Why are big-hill skiers weird about relationships?

Because they're happy when they're on the Rockies!

What did the skier say after she added up the expenses for her trip?

I guess that would summit up!

What happened to the boarder who crashed on the pipe floor?

He was flat-bottom broke!

What do gliders and boarders have in common?

They both love hang time!

⚡☆⚡

Why did the skater pretend that he was someone else?

Because he was working on his fakie!

⚡☆⚡

Why do boarders like to lie on their backs and watch the clouds?

Because they love the big air!

⚡☆⚡

What did people say about the boarder who faceplanted after the big snow?

I guess she needed to powder her nose!

What do boarders call lunch on the hill?

The frost bite!

☆

What do big-hill jumpers like most about their jobs?

The high life!

☆

How did the ski racer sleep at night?

He needed to be all tucked in!

☆

What is it called when two bikers ride together?

A double cross!

☆

Why was the motocross rider so tired in the morning?

Because she needed to be kick-started!

What was the rider doing in the trees?

He had some trouble staying on track!

Where do most racers lose their concentration?

In the whoops!

What do most racers love to listen to on their stereos?

Their own track records!

What did the racers call the pig that tried the course?

A road hog!

✦

Why was the bike racer doing laps around his bed?

He was trying to catch up!

✦

What does a motocross racer do on the track?

About 60 mph!

What color was the catfish the diver saw?

Purrrrple!

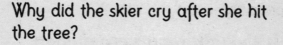

Why couldn't the surfer sleep after having a close encounter with a shark?

He kept having bitemares!

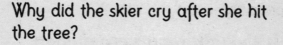

Why did the skier cry after she hit the tree?

It was a weeping willow!

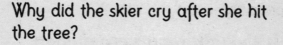

How was the racer's experience crashing through the window?

Very pane-ful!

How did the inline skaters afford their own bowl?

They just pooled their money!

☆

Why did the BMXer get into his dryer?

He just wanted to go for a spin!

☆

What did the owl think about the snowboarders on the pipe?

It thought they were a hoot!

☆

Where did the skater go after the back of her board broke off?

To the re-tail shop, of course!

☆

Why did the boarders get caught by the sudden falling snow?

Because they stopped to ava-lunch!

Why did the racer show up to the course in a suit of armor?

Because he heard that it was a knight race!

What did the boarder say when her friend told her that her nose was running?

No, it snot!

Where do boarders keep their winnings?

In the snowbank!

What did the boarders think after they ran into one another?

They thought it was smashing!

✳✩✳

Why did the diver never trust the jellyfish?

Because he could see right through it!

How did the diver know that he'd come upon some smart fish?

Because they were all still in school!

🐝☆🐝

What did the doctor say about the skier who accidentally swallowed a quarter?

No change yet!

🐝☆🐝

What did the silly biker say when she heard that the new bikes were $300 apiece?

But I want the whole thing!

🐝☆🐝

How did the jellyfish surprise the surfer?

It stung into action!

What did the skater say when he saw sparks coming off the back of his board?

Someone must be hot on my tail!

What did the chairlift operator think about the skiers?

She thought they were a drag!

What did the old boarder call his ancient injuries?

His dino-sores!

What do you call a dangerous deep-sea dive?

An emergen-sea!

Why was the surfer worried about getting water stuck in his ear?

**He thought he might
get brainwashed!**

🐝☆🐝

Why was the boarder so good with her nose tricks?

She knew how to picket!

🐝☆🐝

How did the boarder behave to his buddy who pushed him into the snow?

He gave him the cold shoulder!

🐝☆🐝

What is a good lunch for skiers up on top of a hill?

Ice bergers!

Why was the skater worried about his 11-inch nose?

He thought it might turn into a foot!

🌀☆🌀

Two mountain bikers were lost in the damp clouds. One asked the other where they were. What did his friend say?

I haven't the foggiest idea!

🌀☆🌀

Knock, knock!
Who's there?
Falafel!
Falafel who?
Falafel my skateboard and hurt my knee!

🌀☆🌀

What did the spectator at the downhill race say when asked about the scenery?

I didn't see much. There were all these mountains in front of it!

Why was the boarder crying?

Because he got hit in the eye with a snow bawl!

Why didn't the motocross racer get her dog a license?

Because she knew that they'd never let it compete!

What did the boarder say when he saw the peg-legged pirate on the pipe?

Wooden you know it!

＊

What did the boarder say when her friend commented that her socks didn't match?

I have a pair just like these at home!

＊

What did the dim-witted boarder say when his friend told him that he had put his boots on the wrong feet?

But these are the only feet I have!

＊

Why did the competitive racer stay in bed with a fever of 103°?

He was going for the world record!

Knock, knock!
Who's there?
Bailey!
Bailey who?
Bailey me out of the snow!

What did friends call the racer who crumbled under pressure?

Crackers!

What breakfast cereal do skiers eat?

Flakes!

Why did the lovesick skier wipe out so badly?

Because he was head over heels!

How did the girl and boy boarders know that they'd fallen for each other at the mountain top?

They knew it was love at first height!

Why was the little skater worried about going crazy from having holes in her pockets?

Because she was afraid that she was going to lose her marbles!

🐝☆🐝

What did the boarder say when his father told him that he'd gotten a board for his little sister?

Really? That's an amazing deal!

🐝☆🐝

Knock, knock!
Who's there?
Island!
Island who?
Island perfectly every time I skydive!

🐝☆🐝

Why did the boy tell his father to go sit on the ski hill?

Because his mother wanted a cold pop!

❦☆❦

Why did the BMXer wish that her coach was on the radio?

Because then she could have turned him off!

❦☆❦

What was the surfer named Ace most afraid of?

Card sharks!

❦☆❦

What did the boarder say when he saw his sibling sticking partway out of the snow?

Hey, look, it's my half-brother!

What did the young surfer say about the old surfer who worked at the seafood restaurant?

I can't believe she soled out!

What did the skier say about the snowboarding feline?

Now that's one cool cat!

What do you call the part of a wooden surfboard without holes?

Knot holes!

What did the skaters say when the cops said, "I'll teach you to skate here, young man"?

I wish you would. We keep wiping out!

What did the shark say when it saw the surfers pull up in a Jeep?

Look, canned food!

What did the surfers say while they waited for the tide to come in?

Long time, no sea!

How did the skier feel when he ran into the telephone pole?

He was shocked!

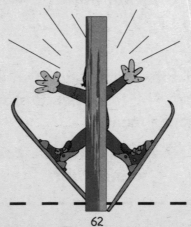

What did the skater say after skating behind a car for a few minutes?

Man, I'm exhausted!

⚡☆⚡

What did the surfboard say to the termite?

Stop boring me!

⚡☆⚡

Why did the surfer bail so big her first time on television?

Because she wanted to make a big splash!

⚡☆⚡

Why did the diver fill his pockets with pencils?

He thought the lead would weigh him down!

Why don't boarders ever wear
watches?

**Because they know
that time flies!**

How does it feel to sit in front of a
fire after skiing all day?

Grate!

Why wasn't the boarder worried
about the icy patches on the pipe?

She thought they were skid stuff!

Why did the motocrosser ride
his bike?

**Because it was too heavy
to carry!**

Why did the hang-glider put his watch on the ground?

He wanted to fly over time!

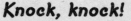

Why did the climber take her watch up the mountain with her?

She wanted to see time travel!

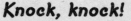

Knock, knock!
Who's there?
Olaf!
Olaf who?
Olaf my skis at the bottom of the hill!

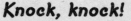

What did the young surfer say to the old surfer who remembered when a phone call cost ten cents?

Hey, dimes have changed!

Did you hear the story about the boarder who snapped the back of her board?

It's a sad tail!

🐝☆🐝

Why did the boarder take a pumpkin off the jump with him?

Because he wanted to make squash!

What did the tired mountain biker say after crashing into the shrubs?

Man, am I bushed!

What did the dirty biker say when it started to rain really hard?

If this keeps up, my name will be mud!

Why did the surfer wipe out?

Because she was blinded by the sunfish!

Why was the surfer so happy to finally get to swim with the dolphins?

Because he felt he really had a porpoise!

What was the highest mountain before Mt. Everest was discovered?

Mt. Everest!

Why are people dumber at the bottom of a chairlift than they are at the top?

Because the crowds are denser down there!

Why didn't the windsurfer believe the story about the piranha attack?

Because it sounded fishy!

Why do boarders love to go up hills?

To get away from being grounded!

How did the boarder feel when he got toasted on the hill?

He was a little burned up about it!

🌀☆🌀

How did the boarder feel when her friend skied right over her?

A little run-down!

🌀☆🌀

How did the little hard-working boarder get such a flat nose?

He kept it to the grindstone!

🌀☆🌀

Why can't army guys be good, relaxed surfers?

Because they're always yelling "Tension!"

How did the blind carpenter make such good boards?

He just picked up his tools and saw!

⚡☆⚡

Why did the big air jumper come down with a cold?

Because her tricks were just too sick!

⚡☆⚡

What do you get when you cross a snowboard with an ax?

The splits!

⚡☆⚡

What did the boarder's dog get?

Trick ticks!

What happened when a pile of snow fell from a bough onto the boarder's head?

It knocked him out cold!

What is the best thing a motocross racer can take when she feels run-down?

The number of the guy who ran over her!

How are pills and hills different?

One is hard to get down and the other is hard to get up!

What is the worst part about BMX bikes for mice?

The squeaking!

What did the boarder get when she cut through the treacherous trees?

A short cut!

What did the cheap racer say when his doctor gave him his bill?

I thought you said you were going to treat me!

How did the boarder feel when he fell into a skier's jacket face first?

Just a little down in the mouth!

How did friends calm down the angry, sunburnt surfer?

They threw a bucket of water on him so he could let off some steam!

What did the sign at the ski slope say?

Laws of Gravity Strictly Enforced!

How did the biker feel after she crashed into the pie shop?

A little crusty!

How did the boarder think he was going to get rich by eating Chinese food?

From the fortune cookies!

What did his friends call the skier after he crashed his new yellow board?

Banana splits!

What did the boarder say after being late because her bank was robbed?

Sorry, I got held up!

Why was the mathematician such a bad surfer in the shark-infested waters?

Because he added four and four and got ate!

How did the boarder spell too much air in two letters?

X-S!

Why were all the fans at the motocross rally wearing white?

Because they were sitting in the bleachers!

How do big-name skaters stay so cool?

They rely on their fans!

What do all BMX bikers have in their shoes?

Athlete's feet!

🌀☆🌀

Why do chilled-out boarders hate tennis so much?

They can't stand the racquet!

🌀☆🌀

Why did the skier like the view in his new goggles?

Because he could see from pole to pole!

🌀☆🌀

How did the biker feel when she got a flat mid-race?

A little deflated!

How did the cheap boarder work out in the off-season?

By pinching pennies!

⚡☆⚡

What did the boarder's dog have to keep it warm?

A fleas (fleece) coat!

⚡☆⚡

How did the surfer feel after too much coffee?

Really perky!

⚡☆⚡

Why did the silly skier get frostbite on his legs?

Because he couldn't figure out how to get the ski pants over his skis!

Why do boarders hate doing laundry
in the winter?

**They're afraid of ring
around the colder!**

☆

What did the boarder call the person
who stole his dog?

A spot remover!

☆

What is bright red and has a trunk?

**A burned surfer heading
home from vacation!**

☆

How do boarders make their
snowpants last?

They put on their jackets first!

How did the skater know that her shoes were tired?

Because their tongues were hanging out!

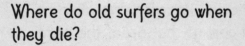

How does a boarder make his bed longer?

He adds his two feet to it!

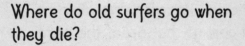

Where do old surfers go when they die?

The Dead Sea!

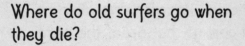

Why did the boarder buy his dog a fur coat?

Because he didn't want it to be a little bare!

Why did the skater think that he
could glide across the country?

**Because he had heard about
a coast-to-coast trip!**

❦✩❦

What did the racer say after she
crossed the dirty finish?

Oh, don't give me that old line!

❦✩❦

What did the boarder sing when he
saw the cow at the top of the pipe?

**The hills are alive with the
sound of mooing!**

❦✩❦

What did the boarder say when she
slipped on a banana skin?

I didn't find that very a-peeling!

What did the towrope say to the boarder?

Hey, can I give you a lift?

How did the biker feel after biking across the archery practice range?

As if he had made an arrow escape!

Why are dogs such bad skaters?

Because they have two left feet—and two right ones!

What game do boarders play when they're bored?

Ride and seek!

☆

What did the chilly boarders sing on New Year's Eve?

Freeze a jolly good fellow!

☆

Why did the skater put her board in the freezer?

Because she wanted to chill out her style!

☆

Why did the BMXer love his hilarious doctor?

Because he kept him in stiches!

Why is it hard to play cards on a windsurfer?

Because you have to stand on the deck!

🌪☆🌪

Why did the climber think that she was going to be in a movie after her accident?

Because she had to be in the cast right away!

🌪☆🌪

Knock, knock!
Who's there?
Snow!
Snow who?
Snow way I'm going rock climbing—it's too dangerous!

🌪☆🌪

Why did the climber in the cast feel like an old record?

He was all scratchy!

❀☆❀

Why is the most famous signature board like Lassie?

Because it's a star with a tail!

❀☆❀

What did the boarder say to his friend William, who was in his way?

Will, you get out of my way!

❀☆❀

Why did the diver begin her dive in shallow water?

Because she wanted to start on a small scale!

How do lost surfers clean their clothes?

They wash ashore!

Why did the old time surfer think he could get his hair done at sea?

He thought he saw a clipper ship!

What did the diver call the fish doctor?

A brain sturgeon!

What did the biker think about crashing into the wall?

It cracked her up!

85

What did the young guys call the old surfer who stood around all day?

The dust collector!

How did the hang glider feel when he crashed into the garbage?

A little down in the dumps!

How did the boarder feel when he crashed into the baker?

A little crumby!

Why didn't the skater trust her new shoes?

Because she thought they were sneakers!

Why didn't the surfer color his own hair?

Because he didn't want to dye!

What did the BMXer think of the dentist who fixed her teeth?

She thought he was boring!

What did the skater think of the man who fixed his shoes?

She thought he was a heel!

What did the boarders think of
the blue-haired boarder with the
big shoes?

They thought he was a clown!

🌪☆🌪

How did the biker feel about the race
after his tire popped?

He felt like he'd blown it!

🌪☆🌪

Why did the boarder wear a cabbage
on her helmet?

*Because she wanted to
get a-head!*

🌪☆🌪

How do late-night bike races start?

On your marks, get set, glow!

Why did the skater throw his Airwalks into the competition bowl?

Because he wanted to be a shoe-in!

What did the boarder think of the pinecones that the squirrels dropped on him?

He thought they were nuts!

What did the diver overhear one fish saying to another?

One of these days, you'll get caught with your mouth open!

What did the biker say to the horse?

Hey, why the long face?

What did the skater say to the curb?

I don't want any of your lip!

🐝☆🐝

Why don't felines surf?

Because they prefer cat-a-marans!

🐝☆🐝

What did the boarders call the longest snowball fight?

The Cold War!

🐝☆🐝

How did the diver try to communicate with the big fish?

She thought she would drop it a line!

🐝☆🐝

What did the muscle-building biker say when he couldn't get a ring out of his bike?

Dumb bell!

What did everyone call the miserly skater who was always wiping out?

Cheapskate!

What did the boarder's cat hate most about walking home after a rainstorm?

The poodles!

What do you call the supporters who are the first up the hill?

Chair leaders!

Why are mountain climbers so bad at Christmas?

They just can't resist a peek!

Why was the poor boarder's dog always chasing its tail?

It was trying to make ends meet!

How did the biker feel after he crashed into the turkey truck?

Pretty stuffed!

🌪☆🌪

What did the hungry surfer feel like after she'd swallowed some salt water?

It just whet her appetite!

🌪☆🌪

What did the boarders call the skeleton who tried to board?

Gutless!

🌪☆🌪

Did you hear about the boarder's fashion crime?

He used a pair of suspenders to hold up his pants!

How can a skier jump off a giant mountain and not get hurt?

She can wait until she gets to the bottom!

🦋☆🦋

How did the surfer fix his banana board?

With his monkey wrench!

🦋☆🦋

What time was it when the climbers came across the bear?

Time to run!

🦋☆🦋

Should a surfer ever swim on a full stomach?

No, he should swim on the ocean!

Why didn't the skiers let any jungle cats race with them?

They thought they were all cheetahs!

☆

Why did the wimpy racer love to send mail?

At least she knew she could lick the stamps!

☆

What did the boarder think when he saw his picture hanging in a window?

He thought he'd been framed!

☆

What did the climber say to his jacket before he went in a cave?

Cover me, I'm going in!

What did the boarder say after she nearly cut herself chopping wood?

That was almost an ax-ident!

⭐

What do BMXers call police officers assigned to the races?

Cop cycles!

⭐

Knock, knock!
Who's there?
Doughnut!
Doughnut who?
Doughnut forget to wear a helmet!

⭐

Why did the skaters stop hanging out with their slingshot-crazy pal?

He was always shooting his mouth off!